Introduction

Marriage by God's Design is a four-session study that examines the Bible's teachings on marriage. Perfect for large or small-group Bible study, this resource can also be used for marriage preparation classes, marriage renewal retreats, or for a parish-wide study on marriage. *Marriage by God's Design* can be led by anyone familiar with the leader guide, participant workbook, and the accompanying DVDs.

The Bible begins with a marriage—Adam and Eve in the Garden of Eden—and ends with a marriage—the marriage feast of Christ and His Bride, the Church. That point cannot be emphasized enough! Throughout its pages, the Bible constantly affirms why God created His human creatures male and female and why He instituted marriage for them. Because *Marriage by God's Design* focuses on the Bible, participants will learn and grow in the understanding and application of its teachings concerning marriage—and single—living.

Marriage by God's Design is built upon the following Bible teachings:

- There is only one God: the Father, the Son, and the Holy Spirit (Deuteronomy 6:4; Matthew 28:19; John 15:26).
- Jesus is the only-begotten Son of God and is our only Savior from sin, Satan, and death (John 1:1–3, 14; 3:16, 36; 17:3; 20:28; 1 John 1:7; 5:20).
- Jesus affirmed God's institution of marriage as recorded in the Bible (Matthew 19:4–6; Mark 10:6–9; Luke 16:18).
- The Bible is God's errorless Word (John 10:35; 1 Timothy 3:16–17; 2 Peter 1:21).
- Marriage is God's institution (Genesis 1:27; 2:24), not a human invention that can be changed according to law, preference, or taste.
- Through God's gift of reason, human beings are able to perceive that God exists (Psalm 19:1; Romans 1:19–20) as well as His will for male and female and marriage (Romans 2:14–15).
- Contemporary psychology and the social sciences provide useful, descriptive information about the human condition, but we are to examine all claims against the truths of the Bible (Acts 17:11; 2 Corinthians 10:5; Colossians 2:8).

Cover photo credits:
© Mika Heittola/Shutterstock, Inc.
© iStockphoto.com
© Shutterstock, Inc.
© mediaphotos/iStockphoto.com
© Jason Stitt/Shutterstock, Inc.
Background © Shutterstock, Inc.

Contents

I0806849

Concordia Publishing House

3558 S. Jefferson Ave.
St. Louis, MO 63118-3968
1-800-325-3040 • www.cph.org

Written by Tim and LeeAnn Radkey, Carl and Heidi Roth, and Robert C. Baker

Edited by Robert C. Baker

This publication may be available in braille, in large print, or on cassette tape for the visually impaired. Please allow 8 to 12 weeks for delivery. Write to Lutheran Blind Mission, 7550 Watson Rd., St. Louis, MO 63119-4409; call toll-free 1-888-215-2455; or visit the Web site: www.blindmission.org.

Manufactured in the United States of America

1 2 3 4 5 6 7 8 9 10
19 18 17 16 15 14 13 12 11 10

Session 1

BUILD

Bible Discovery:

Matthew 19:4–6; Genesis 1:26–28, 31; Hebrews 13:1–5

Objectives: By the power of the Holy Spirit working through God's Word, we will

- learn that Jesus affirmed marriage as the one-flesh union of male and female.
- affirm that God created man and woman in His image.
- confess that God designed marriage to build His human family.
- attest that the devil seeks to destroy marriage in order to undo God's plan of building His human family.
- rejoice that God is restoring His image in us through repentant faith in Christ Jesus, enabling us to affirm marriage.

Male and Female

Bible Discovery

[4][Jesus] answered, "Have you not read that He who created them from the beginning made them male and female, [5]and said, 'Therefore a man shall leave his father and his mother and hold fast to his wife, and the two shall become one flesh'? [6]So they are no longer two but one flesh. What therefore God has joined together, let not man separate." Matthew 19:4–6

What's that Word? Paul notes that when a man and woman become one flesh, they become one in *sōma*, or "body." See 1 Corinthians 6:16. How might this one-flesh, "embodied" view of marriage affect how we evaluate sexual activity before or outside of marriage? divorce? the effort to reconcile husbands and wives?

It's a Miracle! Jesus' first miracle occurred at a wedding. John says that this was the "first" of Jesus' signs manifesting His glory as the Messiah (see John 2:1–11). How does this help us to understand the importance Jesus attaches to marriage? To which future event does this miracle also point us? (Hint: See Revelation 19:6–9.)

Christians love to hear the voice of their Savior, Jesus Christ. In this passage from Matthew 19, which is frequently read at Christian weddings, Jesus speaks to us about marriage. In asking, "Have you not read?" Jesus was responding to a group of pious Jewish teachers, called Pharisees, who wanted Jesus to "take sides" in a theological debate about divorce. However, Jesus understood their intent and took this occasion to affirm marriage by God's design. He did so by quoting the Old Testament Scriptures: Genesis 1, which we'll study in this session, and Genesis 2, which we will study in session 2. This is an especially important point that we'll want to remember throughout this study: Jesus affirms marriage by God's design, and He does so by pointing to the Bible.

Culture Quest The concept of *autonomy* (from two Greek words meaning "self" and "law") is a popular political concept in Western thought. For the past several hundred years, that *political* concept typically applied to states has been *personalized*—we are first and foremost autonomous *individuals* who have *rights* to do or not do certain things.

5. In Jesus' day and in our own, people believe that they have a "right" to marry or a "right" to a divorce for any reason. What are some of our rights as citizens? When may our rights, in fact, be limited? What rights do we have as God's children (see Galatians 4:5)?

6. Using Genesis 2:24, Jesus also teaches that a husband and a wife "leave" father and mother (establish a separate household), "hold fast" to each other (a committed, life-long relationship), and "become" one flesh (exclusive sexual intimacy). If you are married or are preparing for marriage, rank how well you are doing in these areas (1 = need help; 5 = so-so; 10 = doing just fine).

	Physically	Emotionally	Spiritually	Financially
Leave father and mother				
Hold fast to husband or wife				
Become one flesh				

7. When Jesus says, "What therefore God has joined together, let not man separate," He states that *everyone*, not just husband and wife, is responsible for supporting God's institution of marriage. Do you think that most Christians understand that today? Why or why not? What can Christians do to support marriage in our homes? in our churches? in our society?

Marriage in Real Life

8. Matt talks about how he's found marriage with Kathy to be a "safe place." What attitudes and behaviors are important for making marriage "safe"?

9. Dawn talks about being able to "relax" in Rodney's love. How do realistic expectations about oneself and one's spouse contribute to this?

10. David and Sharon suggest that commitment, and not falling in love, is essential for sustainable marriages. Do you think that most people today would agree? Why or why not?

Be Fruitful and Multiply

Bible Discovery

[26]Then God said, "Let Us make man in Our image, after Our likeness. And let them have dominion over the fish of the sea and over the birds of the heavens and over the livestock and over all the earth and over every creeping thing that creeps on the earth."

[27]So God created man in His own image, in the image of God He created him; male and female He created them.

[28]And God blessed them. And God said to them, "Be fruitful and multiply and fill the earth and subdue it and have dominion over the fish of the sea and over the birds of the heavens and over every living thing that moves on the earth." . . . [31]And God saw everything that He had made, and behold, it was very good. And there was evening and there was morning, the sixth day. Genesis 1:26–28, 31

What's that Word? "Image" in Hebrew is *tselem*, which means something patterned after something else. Adam and Eve were created in God's image and likeness, which does not mean that God has a physical body. Rather, Adam and Eve were created in a state of integrity: righteous, holy, and in a state of bodily perfection.

Image Lost, Image Restored Adam and Eve lost God's image because they rebelled against His Word (read the sad story in Genesis 3). God is now restoring His image in those who are forgiven of their sins through faith in His Son, Jesus Christ. See Galatians 3:26–28; Colossians 3:9–10.

One of the most remarkable teachings of the Bible is that God created human beings in His image. This means that, although we are still His human creatures, we are nevertheless unique and have infinite worth over and above God's other creatures. In fact, the coming of Jesus into human flesh and His death for us on the cross proves how much God loves and values His human creatures (John 1:14; 3:16). Think about it: Jesus did not come as an animal, but neither did He come as an angel. Jesus came as one of us: God in human flesh.

Over the years, the Christian Church has defined the "image of God" in different ways. In this course, the image of God is defined as *having spiritual and bodily integrity and completely righteous wills*. This definition of God's image complements four other important Bible teachings: (1) God created Adam and Eve in a state of perfection; (2) Adam and Eve's sin brought God's wrath and His temporal and eternal punishment; (3) we are justified by God's grace through faith in Christ; and (4) by His Word and Spirit, God is restoring His image in us.

Blessed = Enabled Whenever God blesses (Genesis 1:28), He *enables* something to happen according to His will. That children are conceived and born today shows that God's command and blessing of procreation still remain, even after humanity's fall into sin. By sending us His Son, God has proven that He loves His human creation!

11. List ways human beings are

like God	different
____________________	____________________
____________________	____________________
____________________	____________________

like other creatures	different
____________________	____________________
____________________	____________________
____________________	____________________

12. God blesses and commands male and female to "*be fruitful*" and "*multiply*" and "*fill the earth*" and "*subdue it*" and "*have dominion*" (Genesis 1:28, emphasis added). Take a good look at the italicized words in this passage. If God were an architect and if marriage were His blueprint, what would God be building? What does the devil do to undo God's "building project"?

____

____

____

____

Marriage in Real Life

13. Norma emphasizes how important trust is in marriage. How can husbands and wives build trust in their relationship?

14. Kathy and Tom suggest that marriage takes a lot of work and that part of that work is forgiveness. How important is forgiveness in any relationship?

15. David says that serving their wives sacrificially, husbands become more like Christ, who serves His Church. In what ways can the Church emphasize that teaching?

Honoring Marriage

Bible Discovery

[1]Let brotherly love continue. [2]Do not neglect to show hospitality to
strangers, for thereby some have entertained angels unawares. [3]Remember
those who are in prison, as though in prison with them, and those who are
mistreated, since you also are in the body. [4]Let marriage be held in honor
among all, and let the marriage bed be undefiled, for God will judge the
sexually immoral and adulterous. [5]Keep your life free from love of money,
and be content with what you have, for He has said, "I will never leave you
nor forsake you." Hebrews 13:1–5

What's that Word? Hebrews 13:4 says that marriage is to be held by all in "honor," in Greek *timios*, which means "precious" or "valuable." As an adjective, the word is used to refer to the "precious blood of Christ" (1 Peter 1:19). Even as we honor Christ's precious blood shed for our salvation, we honor God's gift of marriage.

What's that Word? Hebrews 13:4 says that God will punish the "sexually immoral and adulterous," *pornous* and the *moichous*—fornicators and adulterers. These Greek terms refer to those who are actively involved in illicit sexual activity. A fornicator is unmarried; an adulterer is married. Both commit sexually immoral deeds outside of God's design for marriage.

16. Discuss the ways that Christians—whether single, married, or single again—can honor marriage according to God's design.

Closing Prayer

Almighty God, you created man and woman in Your image. Grant that all men and women—whether whether single, married, or single again—would be recreated in Your image through repentant faith in Jesus Christ. Send Your Holy Spirit so that we might be enabled to live holy lives according to Your Word. We ask this in Jesus' name. Amen.

This Week:

- Exercise is good for the body and the soul. What three things can you do this week to keep your relationships (whether with your spouse, kids, friends, or neighbors) healthy?
- The devil often uses little things to cause huge divisions between us and those we love. With God's help, what practical steps can you take to focus on the big picture?
- The last time you and a loved one had a laugh, what was it about? Share that with him or her the next time you talk or see each other.

Session 2

LOVE

Bible Discovery:

Matthew 19:10–12; 1 Corinthians 7:8–17; Genesis 2:15–24; Ephesians 5:21–33

Objectives: By the power of the Holy Spirit working through God's Word, we will

- learn that Jesus affirmed God's exemption of some people from the married state.
- affirm that God blesses some people to a lifetime of chaste singleness for the sake of His kingdom.
- confess that God designed marriage as the centerpiece of human love.
- attest that the devil seeks to destroy marriage in order to destroy human society.
- rejoice that Christ lovingly sacrificed His life for us in order to transform us into His Bride, the Church.

© Shutterstock, Inc.

Marriage in the Media: Single-parent Families

Match the following:

1. Michael and son, George Michael, try to keep it together despite Michael's father's arrest and assorted Bluth and Fünke family dyfunctions.
2. Stars Hollow is a peaceful town, but for Lorelai and her daughter, Rory, Friday night dinners with Lorelai's parents can be a little tense.
3. Ann Romano works and cares for daughters Julie and Barbara; when he's not hitting on her, building super Schneider tries to help.
4. Without the impeccable Mr. French, Bill Davis would be challenged by teenager Cissy, twins Buffy and Jody, and Mrs. Beasley.
5. After James's untimely death, times weren't always "dyn-o-mite" in Chicago for Florida Evans and children J.J., Thelma, and Michael.
6. Dad Robby Ray has his hands full managing the pop-star status of daughter Miley's famous alter ego—that, and son Jackson's poor grades.

a. *Family Affair*
b. *Good Times*
c. *Gilmore Girls*
d. *Hannah Montana*
e. *One Day at a Time*
f. *Arrested Development*

Answers: 1 f; 2 c; 3 e; 4 a; 5 b; 6 d.

1. The media often portrays single parents as struggling to earn a living while trying to manage a household. In what ways is this portrayal accurate? In what ways do married parents share the same struggles?

____

____

____

____

Marriage in Real Life

2. Single again after twenty-six years, Norma says that we "can get through anything" because Jesus is by our side. When does this seem easy to believe? difficult?

3. Having lost Linda to ALS (Lou Gerhig's disease), Carl still believes marriage is "worth it." How is the biblical view of marriage still important for singles—and those who are single again?

4. Carmon suggests that ministry to singles is a two-way street: the Church needs to reach out to singles, but singles also need to try to stay connected. How is your congregation connecting with singles? those who are single again?

What about Singles?

Bible Discovery

10The disciples said to him, "If such is the case of a man with his wife, it
is better not to marry." 11But He said to them, "Not everyone can receive
this saying, but only those to whom it is given. 12For there are eunuchs
who have been so from birth, and there are eunuchs who have been
made eunuchs by men, and there are eunuchs who have made themselves
eunuchs for the sake of the kingdom of heaven. Let the one who is able
to receive this receive it." Matthew 19:10–12

What's that Word? Jesus uses the Greek word *eunouchoi* ("eunuchs," v. 12) to refer to those who have an impediment to marriage and those who have chosen to live chaste, single lives in service to the Lord. (Note: By itself, the inability to have children *does not exclude* a man or woman from entering marriage.)

What's that Word? What is Paul's advice to unmarried persons and those who have lost their spouse? Stay single (1 Corinthians 6:8–9)! However, for those who "cannot exercise self-control," it is better to quench the flames of sexual desire in holy marriage than to *purousthai*, "burn with passion" (v. 9).

Matthew 19:10–12 describes a brief, and probably private, conversation between Jesus and His disciples following His encounter with the Pharisees. A paraphrase of the disciples' response in verse 10 might go something like this: "If sexual unfaithfulness is the only legitimate ground for divorce, then perhaps it is better to remain single." Their response is instructive on two counts. First, since Jesus does not correct them, it shows that the disciples had understood Jesus' teaching concerning legitimate divorce. Second, whereas the Pharisees were asking Jesus to justify getting out of an existing marriage, His disciples expressed concern about avoiding marriage altogether.

Jesus' response to the Pharisees and His disciples was uncompromising. God joins a husband and his wife together in marriage (Matthew 19:6), therefore they should remain in marriage. Likewise, God gives a special gift of celibacy for the sake of His kingdom "only those to whom it is given" (Matthew 19:11). Therefore, married couples should not seek to divorce, and single persons should not try to avoid marriage unless God has given them the special gift of celibacy. Here, Jesus teaches that every person should be thankful and accept whatever station in life God places us—married or single. (See also Paul's discussion of abandonment by an unbelieving spouse in 1 Corinthians 7:15.)

God, Widows, and Orphans

James writes, "Religion that is pure and undefiled before God, the Father, is this: to visit orphans and widows in their affliction, and to keep oneself unstained from the world" (1:27). How might we better serve adults who have lost a spouse and children who have lost a parent?

5. In the columns below, list the advantages of being married and of being single.

Advantages of being married	Advantages of being single
______________________	______________________
______________________	______________________
______________________	______________________

6. Our Western culture prizes personal independence, self-reliance, and choice. Do you think that these values make it more difficult to accept our God-given stations in life—whether married or single? Why or why not? How can knowing that our lives are in God's hands help?

____

____

____

____

Marriage in Real Life

7. Tim thinks globally, while Lisa concentrates more on details. In what other ways do we see that marriage is the union of a *complementary* pair—male and female, husband and wife?

8. Dawn suggests that husbands and wives should not expect their spouse to fulfill all their emotional needs. Do you agree or disagree? Rodney suggests that being with other Christians couples who are "working on their marriage" can help. How so?

9. Glenn talks about being united in making decisions, while Patti talks more about being sensitive to each other's emotional needs. How are both intellectual and emotional growth important in marriage?

Bible Discovery

8 Now to the unmarried and the widows I say that it is good for them to
remain single as I am. 9 But if they cannot exercise self-control, they should
marry. For it is better to marry than to burn with passion.

10 To the married I give this charge (not I, but the Lord): the wife should
not separate from her husband 11 (but if she does, she should remain
unmarried or else be reconciled to her husband), and the husband should
not divorce his wife.

12 To the rest I say (I, not the Lord) that if any brother has a wife who is an
unbeliever, and she consents to live with him, he should not divorce her.
13 If any woman has a husband who is an unbeliever, and he consents to
live with her, she should not divorce him. 14 For the unbelieving husband
is made holy because of his wife, and the unbelieving wife is made holy
because of her husband. Otherwise your children would be unclean, but
as it is, they are holy. 15 But if the unbelieving partner separates, let it be so.
In such cases the brother or sister is not enslaved. God has called you to
peace. 16 For how do you know, wife, whether you will save your husband?
Or how do you know, husband, whether you will save your wife?

17 Only let each person lead the life that the Lord has assigned to him,
and to which God has called him. This is the rule in all the churches.
1 Corinthians 7:8–17

10. In this passage, Paul distinguishes between the Lord's commands and his own apostolic and pastoral counsel. Remember that Paul was writing under the inspiration of the Holy Spirit (see 2 Timothy 3:16–17; 2 Peter 1:21). His counsel is not mere "advice," but rather the application of authoritative scriptural truth. Distinguish between command and counsel.

	Command	Counsel
Remain single if you can exercise sexual self-control.	________	________
Marry if you cannot exercise sexual self-control.	________	________
A wife should not separate from her husband.	________	________
A husband should not divorce his wife.	________	________
Remain married to an unbelieving spouse.	________	________

When Paul commends singleness as "better" (1 Corinthians 7:38), he means that single persons are likely to have more time for prayer, teaching, and service, as Jesus says, "for the sake of the kingdom of heaven" (Matthew 19:12). Paul writes that single Christians can be "anxious about the things of the Lord, how to please the Lord . . . how to be holy in body and spirit" (1 Corinthians 7:32, 34) while married Christians legitimately are often "anxious about worldly things," such as serving their spouses, providing for their families, and so on (vv. 33–34). Remember that all of life is a gift from the Lord, and "everything created by God is good, and nothing is to be rejected if it is received with thanksgiving, for it is made holy by the word of God and prayer" (1 Timothy 4:4–5).

Marriage in Real Life

11. Lisa talks about how she learned to trust Tim with paying the bills while she was experiencing a difficult pregnancy. Why is trust so important, especially during tough times?

____
____
____
____

12. Kathy says that God "was so sweet" because Tom was the first person she saw following her successful surgery. In what other ways can spouses experience God's "sweetness" through each other?

____
____
____
____

13. David and Sharon emphasize how good and regular communication is an "investment in each other." What "dividends" might a couple realize when they communicate often—and well?

____
____
____
____

They Will Become One Flesh

Bible Discovery

15 The LORD God took the man and put him in the garden of Eden to
work it and keep it. 16 And the LORD God commanded the man, saying,
"You may surely eat of every tree of the garden, 17 but of the tree of the
knowledge of good and evil you shall not eat, for in the day that you eat
of it you shall surely die."

18 Then the LORD God said, "It is not good that the man should be alone;
I will make him a helper fit for him." 19 Now out of the ground the LORD
God had formed every beast of the field and every bird of the heavens and
brought them to the man to see what he would call them. And whatever
the man called every living creature, that was its name. 20 The man gave
names to all livestock and to the birds of the heavens and to every beast
of the field. But for Adam there was not found a helper fit for him. 21 So
the LORD God caused a deep sleep to fall upon the man, and while he
slept took one of his ribs and closed up its place with flesh. 22 And the rib
that the LORD God had taken from the man he made into a woman and
brought her to the man. 23 Then the man said,

"This at last is bone of my bones and flesh of my flesh; she shall be called Woman, because she was taken out of Man."

24 Therefore a man shall leave his father and his mother and hold fast to
his wife, and they shall become one flesh. Genesis 2:15–24

What's that Word? *Ezer kenegdō* in Hebrew means "a helper fit for him" (Genesis 2:18, 20). In the Old Testament, "helper" often refers to God's relationship toward Israel, as in "Our help is in the name of the LORD, who made heaven and earth" (Psalm 124:8). This shows that a "helper" plays a vital role in the well-being of someone else.

What's that Word? In Hebrew, "hold fast" (v. 24), *davak* means "to be joined" or to "cling to." Marriage is more than a mere legal agreement that can be contracted or dissolved by mutual consent. Rather, God joins man and wife in marriage (Matthew 19:6), which is the lifelong, one-flesh union of husband and wife.

Genesis 2:15–24 provides additional details about the creation of man that are not given in 1:26–31. "Not good" (v. 18) does not mean that Adam was evil or morally faulty, but incomplete. Adam needed a complementary partner of the opposite sex. Eve was the fit helper God made for Adam from his own body. God created male and female to complete each other as "one flesh" in the marital union. Only after the pinnacle of God's creation—man and woman—were created was the creation "very good" (Genesis 1:31).

14. In Genesis 2:22–24, the Bible describes the very first wedding! Thinking of today's wedding party (bride, groom, best man, maid or matron of honor, and so on), which role or roles did God play at Adam and Eve's wedding? Be sure that Jesus' words influence your answer: "What therefore God has joined together, let not man separate" (Matthew 19:6).

____

____

____

____

15. The first recorded human words in the Bible are Adam's words of awe about Eve: "This at last is bone of my bones and flesh of my flesh; she shall be called Woman, because she was taken out of Man" (v. 23). How did Adam recognize similarities between himself and Eve? How did he recognize differences?

____

____

____

____

Loving Submission, Loving Service

Bible Discovery

. . . [21]submitting to one another out of reverence for Christ.

[22]Wives, submit to your own husbands, as to the Lord. [23]For the husband
is the head of the wife even as Christ is the head of the church, His body,
and is Himself its Savior. [24]Now as the church submits to Christ, so also
wives should submit in everything to their husbands.

[25]Husbands, love your wives, as Christ loved the church and gave Himself
up for her, [26]that He might sanctify her, having cleansed her by the
washing of water with the word, [27]so that He might present the church to
Himself in splendor, without spot or wrinkle or any such thing, that she
might be holy and without blemish. [28]In the same way husbands should
love their wives as their own bodies. He who loves his wife loves himself.
[29]For no one ever hated his own flesh, but nourishes and cherishes it,
just as Christ does the church, [30]because we are members of His body.
[31]"Therefore a man shall leave his father and mother and hold fast to his
wife, and the two shall become one flesh." [32]This mystery is profound, and
I am saying that it refers to Christ and the church. [33]However, let each one
of you love his wife as himself, and let the wife see that she respects her
husband. Ephesians 5:21–33

What's that Word? "Submit" comes from the Greek word *hupotassō*, which suggests being subordinate to someone else. Christians submit to one another (v. 21); wives submit to their husbands (v. 22); and the Church submits to Christ (v. 24). In addition, husbands are to love their wives self-sacrificially as Christ loved the Church (v. 26).

What's that Word? One of the Greek words for "love" is *agape*, which is used as a verb in John 3:16—"For God so loved the world." Agape is God's special, perfect love that is ours only by His grace in Christ. Paul uses a verb form of *agape* when he describes Christ's love for the Church and a husband's love for his wife. God calls all husbands to actively pursue their wives' well-being, just as Christ did for His Bride, the Church.

Contemporary notions of romantic love often conflict with the description of love in the Bible. The love that God has for us, the love that Christ has for the Church, the love that husbands should have for their wives is *agape* love, a kind of love whose source is God Himself. *Agape* love doesn't work for the benefit of the lover, but for the beloved. That's the kind of love husbands should have for their wives. When husbands love their wives in this self-sacrificial way, it is easier for wives to "submit" to and "respect" their husbands, as the Bible says (Ephesians 5:22, 33).

16. "God shows His love for us in that while we were still sinners, Christ died for us" (Romans 5:8). "We love because He first loved us" (1 John 4:19). How can these verses bring renewal to those regretting unloving words and actions toward those they love?

____

____

____

Closing Prayer

Lord Jesus Christ, You call all of your disciples, single and married alike, to live chaste and holy lives. Grant us strength to resist sexual temptation, and help us to live in purity before You. Bless husbands, wives, children, and those who are single, for You have purchased and won us by Your precious blood and have made us Your Bride, Your pure and holy Church. In Your name we pray. Amen.

This Week:

- What three things can you do this week to show your love and care for your spouse or, if you're single, a family member or friend?
- Discuss one area of your relationship that needs improvement and name the future benefits of such an improvement. Prayerfully ask God for help in putting that into practice.
- The next time you are at fault, say, "Please forgive me for" and name your fault. And if a loved one confesses a fault to you, respond by saying, "I forgive you for Jesus' sake."

Session 3

PROTECT

Bible Discovery:

1 Corinthians 7:2–7; Matthew 5:27–28, 31–32; 1 Timothy 1:8–11; 4:1–5; Romans 12:1–2; 1 Thessalonians 4:3–8; 1 Corinthians 6:9–11

Objectives: By the power of the Holy Spirit working through God's Word, we will

- learn that after the fall of Adam and Eve, God added another purpose to marriage: to restrain sin.
- affirm that sexual sins, like all sins, begin in the human heart.
- attest that the devil seeks to destroy marriage through sexual temptation and false teaching about marriage.
- rejoice that God's mercy in Christ renews our minds and hearts so that we may offer Him our bodies in holiness and purity.
- give thanks for the radical, transforming nature of God's grace and forgiveness in Jesus Christ.

Marriage in the Media: Blended Families

Match the following:

1. Deliveryman Doug's crazy schemes and legal assistant Carrie's biting wit can't beat Carrie's wacky, basement-dwelling dad, Arthur.
2. Mike and Carol have their hands and house full with Greg, Peter, Bobby, Marcia, Jan, and Cindy—and don't forget housekeeper Alice.
3. Frank and Carol's Jamaican wedding means that unlikely siblings Dana, Karen, Mark, J.T., Al, and Brendan take things one step at a time.
4. With mom, Nora, and sister, Lizzie, Casey has to adjust to a new life with a stepfather and stepsiblings—and one stepbrother in particular.
5. Once married, now divorced, Lily Manning and Rick Sammler are dating again; and then there are kids Grace, Zoe, Eli, and Jessie.
6. Dad Jay is married to a younger woman, daughter Claire is a homemaker, and son Mitchell has a new baby—with boyfriend Cameron.

a. *Step by Step*
b. *Modern Family*
c. *Life With Derek*
d. *Once and Again*
e. *The Brady Bunch*
f. *The King of Queens*

Answers: 1 f; 2 e; 3 a; 4 c; 5 d; 6 b.

1. Today's "situation comedy" has its roots in vaudeville and early radio programs. In what ways do comedic situations help us to explore difficult issues or topics, especially those we face in marriage and families?

____

____

____

____

Marriage in Real Life

2. Ken and Amy stress how compromise is important in marriage. What are some things that husbands and wives should never compromise? What are some things they can compromise?

3. Tim and Lisa emphasize the importance of husbands and wives praying *with* each other and praying *for* each other. Why are both important?

4. Kathy shares how Matt has helped her to recognize that "we'll get through it." Such confidence is borne by faith. What faith-building activities can husbands and wives enjoy together?

Each Should Have a Spouse

Bible Discovery

2But because of the temptation to sexual immorality, each man should
have his own wife and each woman her own husband. 3The husband
should give to his wife her conjugal rights, and likewise the wife to her
husband. 4For the wife does not have authority over her own body, but
the husband does. Likewise the husband does not have authority over his
own body, but the wife does. 5Do not deprive one another, except perhaps
by agreement for a limited time, that you may devote yourselves to prayer;
but then come together again, so that Satan may not tempt you because of
your lack of self-control. 6Now as a concession, not a command, I say this.
7I wish that all were as I myself am. But each has his own gift from God,
one of one kind and one of another. 1 Corinthians 7:2–7

More Important! In sessions 1 and 2, we learned that God designed marriage to build His human family and to be the centerpiece of human love between husband and wife. In 1 Corinthians 7:2–7, Paul notes that because of the fall into sin, marriage has become even *more important* because of sexual temptation.

Bible Discovery

27"You have heard that it was said, 'You shall not commit adultery.' 28But
I say to you that everyone who looks at a woman with lustful intent has
already committed adultery with her in his heart. . . . 31It was also said,
'Whoever divorces his wife, let him give her a certificate of divorce.' 32But
I say to you that everyone who divorces his wife, except on the ground
of sexual immorality, makes her commit adultery, and whoever marries a
divorced woman commits adultery." Matthew 5:27–28, 31–32

What's that Word? "Commit adultery" in the Greek is *moicheuō*, the sin forbidden in the Sixth Commandment. Jesus expands the category of sexual sins to include even looking at someone "with lustful intent" (Matthew 5:28). All sexual sins of thought, word, and deed fall under the prohibition of the Sixth Commandment.

Movies, television, the Internet, radio, print media, and billboards bombard our eyes and ears with sexual images and talk about sex. That our society is so saturated with sexual immorality proves that our hearts are "deceitful above all things, and desperately sick; who can understand [them]?" (Jeremiah 17:9).

However, we would be wrong to conclude that God is against the proper and natural sexual relations between husband and wife—far from it! The beautiful refrains of the lover and the beloved in Song of Solomon dispel such a view: "Behold, you are beautiful, my love; behold, you are beautiful; your eyes are doves. Behold, you are beautiful, my beloved, truly delightful. Our couch is green" (Song of Solomon 1:15–16).

Here we see the beauty, passion, and romance that God designed to be enjoyed by husband and wife in marriage. In fact, as Paul argues in 1 Corinthians 7:2–7, due to the humankind's fall into sin, marriage serves another purpose: by providing a natural channel to focus sexual desire, marriage protects us from sexual immorality. Natural sexual intercourse, as God designed it, is good and useful and—when enjoyed by a repentant and believing husband and wife—holy (see 1 Timothy 4:4–6).

5. Review Genesis 1:28; 2:24. Along with 1 Corinthians 7:2, now list the three reasons God has given natural sexual intercourse to husband and wife:

   Genesis 1:28 ______________________________

   Genesis 2:24 ______________________________

   1 Corinthians 7:2 ______________________________

Marriage in Real Life

6. Matt and Kathy express how they have learned responsibility, consistency, and compassion in their marriage. What other virtues can husbands and wives learn from each other?

7. Dawn mentions how non-Christian values distract us from the gifts that God gives in marriage. What are some of those values and how can we guard against their influence?

8. Glenn quotes Ecclesiastes 4:12: "A threefold cord is not quickly broken." How can that be applied to a Christian marriage, knowing that the "third cord" is our Savior, Jesus Christ?

Law for the Lawless

Bible Discovery

8Now we know that the law is good, if one uses it lawfully, 9understanding
this, that the law is not laid down for the just but for the lawless and
disobedient, for the ungodly and sinners, for the unholy and profane, for
those who strike their fathers and mothers, for murderers, 10the sexually
immoral, men who practice homosexuality, enslavers, liars, perjurers, and
whatever else is contrary to sound doctrine, 11in accordance with the
gospel of the glory of the blessed God with which I have been entrusted.
1 Timothy 1:8–11

Culture Quest

Today, some Christians try to justify same-sex sexual activity by maintaining that Paul did not understand the causes of same-sex attraction. However, in 1 Corinthians 6:9, Paul uses two Greek technical terms, *arsenokoitai* and *malakoi*, which refer to active and passive same-sex sexual partners. Clearly Paul understood—and condemned—the practice.

What's that Word?

In Romans 1:26–27, Paul uses a Greek phrase, *phusikēn chrēsin*, which can be translated as "natural function." God designed the male and female bodies to "function" properly together in marriage. Same-sex sexual activity militates against our bodies' proper "function," marriage, and, ultimately, God Himself.

When God created Adam and Eve, he created them in His image: with holy and righteous wills. God stamped His holy Law onto their hearts (Romans 2:14–15). When they sinned, that holiness and righteousness was lost, but humankind still has an internal, natural sense of right and wrong, although that sense is corrupted. God's revealed Law (the Ten Commandments) now serves primarily to show us our sin and our need for a Savior (Romans 3:20; 1 Timothy 1:9). Although we are now holy and righteous through faith and are being renewed in Christ's image (Ephesians 4:24, Colossians 3:10), the Law keeps our sinful flesh in check (Romans 6:6; Ephesians 4:22; Colossians 3:9). Jesus Christ has set us free from the Law's condemnation and the penalty our sinful flesh deserves (Romans 7:24–25a). We can join Paul in saying, "Thanks be to God though Jesus Christ our Lord!" (v. 25).

9. In 1 Timothy 1:9–10, Paul recites the Ten Commandments to show how we all have violated God's Law. Match Paul's words in this passage (numbers) to the commandments as drawn from Exodus 20 (letters).

1. the lawless and disobedient	a. Do not have other gods (Exodus 20:3).	______
2. ungodly and sinners	b. Do not take God's name in vain (v. 7).	______
3. unholy and profane	c. Keep the Sabbath day holy (v. 8).	______
4. those who strike their fathers and mothers	d. Honor your father and mother (v. 12).	______
5. murderers	e. Do not murder (v. 13).	______
6. the sexually immoral	f. Do not commit adultery (v. 14).	______
7. men who practice homosexuality	g. Do not steal (v. 15).	______
8. enslavers (those who "steal" people)	h. Do not bear false witness (v. 16).	______
9. liars, perjurers	i Do not covet neighbor's house (v. 17).	______
10. whatever else is contrary to sound doctrine	j. Do not covet your neighbor's wife (v. 17).	______

Bible Discovery

1 Now the Spirit expressly says that in later times some will depart from the
faith by devoting themselves to deceitful spirits and teachings of demons,
2 through the insincerity of liars whose consciences are seared, 3 who
forbid marriage and require abstinence from foods that God created to
be received with thanksgiving by those who believe and know the truth.
4 For everything created by God is good, and nothing is to be rejected if it
is received with thanksgiving, 5 for it is made holy by the word of God and
prayer. 1 Timothy 4:1–5

Proper and Natural Some Christians give the impression that God condemns only certain sexual sins. However, *all* sexual sins are sins against our bodies (1 Corinthians 6:18). God's stringent rules for the proper and natural use of our bodies are meant for *everyone* and are designed to protect not only marriage, but also our relationship with Him.

10. In 1 Timothy 4:1–5, Paul notes that in the latter days, "liars whose consciences are seared" (v. 2) will teach falsely about marriage, food, and other good gifts that God has created for the enjoyment of His people. What are the results of this false teaching based on the examples below?

False teaching:	Results:
Forbidding marriage to Church leaders	____________________
Same-sex marriage	____________________
Unscriptural divorce	____________________
Forbidding certain food or drink	____________________

Marriage in Real Life

11. Kathy notes that she learned the importance of confession (admitting our sins) and absolution (forgiving each other in Jesus' name) in marriage from Matt. Which do you think is harder to do? Why?

____

____

____

12. Patti and Glenn mention the importance of private Bible reading and prayer and corporate worship. Besides the hope, joy, and peace that Patti mentions, what are additional benefits of being in God's Word?

____

____

____

____

13. David emphasizes having an "ongoing conversation" with Jesus. What can we do to extend worship (God's Word, prayer, hymns, and so on) into our day-to-day activities?

____

____

____

____

You Were Washed

Bible Discovery

[1]I appeal to you therefore, brothers, by the mercies of God, to present
your bodies as a living sacrifice, holy and acceptable to God, which is your
spiritual worship. [2]Do not be conformed to this world, but be transformed
by the renewal of your mind, that by testing you may discern what is the
will of God, what is good and acceptable and perfect. Romans 12:1–2

What's that Word? "Sacrifice" (Romans 12:1) in Greek is *thusia*, which reminds us of Jesus' sacrifice for us on the cross. "Christ loved us and gave Himself up for us, a fragrant offering and sacrifice to God" (Ephesians 5:2). Jesus' bodily sacrifice for us enables us to offer our bodies to God as spiritual sacrifices in thanksgiving.

14. Paul makes his appeal for holy living based on "the mercies of God" (Romans 12:1) that are ours in Jesus Christ. What is the connection between the "renewal of [our minds]" (v. 2) and the spiritual sacrifice and worship we make with our bodies?

Bible Discovery

[3]For this is the will of God, your sanctification: that you abstain from
sexual immorality; [4]that each one of you know how to control his own
body in holiness and honor, [5]not in the passion of lust like the Gentiles
who do not know God; [6]that no one transgress and wrong his brother in
this matter, because the Lord is an avenger in all these things, as we told
you beforehand and solemnly warned you. [7]For God has not called us for
impurity, but in holiness. [8]Therefore whoever disregards this, disregards not
man but God, who gives His Holy Spirit to you. 1 Thessalonians 4:3–8

What's that Word? In 1 Thessalonians 4:4, the Greek word translated as "body" is *skeuos*, which means "vessel," "implement," or "goods." Here, Paul refers delicately to the sex organs. In Christ, God sets us free from the power of the sinful nature and gives us control over our bodies and each of their individual parts.

15. God gives us His Holy Spirit so that we might be sanctified in holy living. Too often, however, our lives are anything but holy. However, "the blood of Jesus cleanses us from all sin" (1 John 1:7). What additional promises do you find in 1 John 1:8–9?

____

____

____

____

Bible Discovery

9 Or do you not know that the unrighteous will not inherit the kingdom
of God? Do not be deceived: neither the sexually immoral, nor idolaters,
nor adulterers, nor men who practice homosexuality, 10 nor thieves, nor the
greedy, nor drunkards, nor revilers, nor swindlers will inherit the kingdom
of God. 11 And such were some of you. But you were washed, you were
sanctified, you were justified in the name of the Lord Jesus Christ and by
the Spirit of our God. 1 Corinthians 6:9–11

What's that Word? The Greek word for "were," ēte, in 1 Corinthians 6:11 emphasizes that the baptized are *no longer* immoral, idolaters, adulterers, and so forth. They receive a new identification and a new lifestyle in Jesus Christ, their Savior. What Good News for those who want to "wash away" their old lifestyles and the guilt of sin!

16. Focusing on verse 11, fill in the blanks. Baptized "in the name of the Lord Jesus Christ and by the Spirit of our God"

you were "__________________" (cleansed of your sins)

you were "__________________" (made holy)

you were "__________________" (declared in a right relationship with God for Christ's sake)

Closing Prayer

Almighty Father, for our sins of thought, word, and deed, we justly deserve Your punishment. For the sake of Your Son, Jesus Christ, forgive us. Send Your Holy Spirit to renew our hearts and minds, so that we may lead pure and decent lives in all that we say and do. We ask this through Christ, our Lord. Amen.

This Week:

- Make a list of the virtues of someone you love, and use that list to compose a card, letter, e-mail, or text and send it to your loved one. Start off with, "I love you because . . . "
- Make a note of when or under what circumstances you are most vulnerable to sexual temptation. Ask God—and a close friend—to help you during those times.
- While you still may be sorely tempted, you no longer belong to your sins. Rejoice that God placed His name *on* you—Father, Son, and Holy Spirit—and His Spirit *within* you!

Session 4

TEACH

Bible Discovery:

Luke 18:15–17; Psalm 127:3–5; Deuteronomy 6:4–9; Psalm 78:4–7; Romans 8:14–17

Objectives: By the power of the Holy Spirit working through God's Word, we will

- learn that Jesus welcomes all people into God's kingdom regardless of age or ability.
- affirm that God gives children as a gift so that by His grace they may become citizens of His kingdom through faith.
- confess that God designed marriage in order to teach future generations about His grace and blessing in Christ.
- attest that the devil seeks to destroy marriage in order to rob future generations of the gift of faith.
- rejoice that through the Gospel of Jesus Christ, the Holy Spirit has called us to an eternal relationship with God, our heavenly Father.

Marriage in the Media: Wacky Families

Match the following:

1. Jed, Granny, Elly Mae, and Jethro keep their critters and cook their vittles in their mansion next door to their banker, Mr. Drysdale.
2. While Morticia and Gomez are passionate, Wednesday, Pugsley, Fester, Grandmama, Lurch, Thing, and Cousin Itt are just plain creepy.
3. Although she swore off using her magical powers, Samantha occasionally casts a spell to keep her mortal husband, Darrin, out of trouble.
4. Fresh from Philly, Will learns to adapt to upper-crust California living with Uncle Philip and Aunt Vivian—and English butler Geoffrey.
5. Although he's a scheming, loudmouthed, hot-tempered bus driver, Ralph is moonstruck over his honey, Alice—and he's Ed's buddy.
6. Cranky Thelma and her high-strung sister, Fran, open their doors to Vint, Buzz, and Sonja; later, pretentious neighbor Naomi moves in too.

a. *The Fresh Prince of Bel-Air*
b. *The Beverly Hillbillies*
c. *Mama's Family*
d. *The Honeymooners*
e. *Bewitched*
f. *The Addams Family*

Answers: 1 b; 2 f; 3 e; 4 a; 5 d; 6 c.

1. What things do you or your family do that your neighbors might find a little out of the ordinary or even a bit wacky? Share if you dare!

____

____

____

____

Marriage in Real Life

2. Matt and Kathy find a lot of their own personality traits, which are inherited, in their children. What characteristics, values, or habits do children *learn* from their parents?

3. Dawn mentions how she and Rodney learned from their children. How does God use parenthood, like marriage, to conform us to be more like Christ?

4. Patti and Glenn enjoy their grandchildren. Besides parents and grandparents, who else has the opportunity to teach children about God's love and grace?

Let the Children Come to Me

Bible Discovery

15 Now they were bringing even infants to Him that He might touch them.
And when the disciples saw it, they rebuked them. 16 But Jesus called them
to Him, saying, "Let the children come to Me, and do not hinder them,
for to such belongs the kingdom of God. 17 Truly, I say to you, whoever
does not receive the kingdom of God like a child shall not enter it."
Luke 18:15–17

What's that Word? "Infants" (Luke 18:15) in the Greek is *brephē*, a broad term that includes newborns all the way to toddlers. When it comes to God's kingdom, Jesus does not discriminate based on age or ability. In fact, Jesus says we receive God's kingdom with infantile faith—faith that God gives us as a gift (see Ephesians 2:8–9).

Jesus loves the little children, All the children of the world;
Red and yellow, black and white, They are precious in His sight.
Jesus loves the little children of the world.
Clare Herbert Woolston (1856–1927; public domain)

So far in *Marriage by God's Design*, we've learned that God designed marriage to (1) build His human family; (2) provide a place where husband and wife can serve each other in love; and (3) protect His children from temptation and the dangers of sexual sin. In this fourth and final session, we will learn that God also designed marriage as the place where children are taught and grow in the Christian faith.

What is Jesus' attitude about children? He loves them! He invites them. He welcomes them. He blesses them. In fact, as this passage from Luke 18 reveals, Jesus loves children so much that He rebuked His disciples for trying to keep these little ones from Him. This passage reminds us of another occurrence when Jesus used children to teach His disciples: "Whoever receives this child in My name receives Me, and whoever receives Me receives Him who sent Me" (Luke 9:46–48). Indeed, Jesus loves the little children of the world.

5. In this passage, parents were bringing their children to Jesus in order for Him to bless them through His touch. Make a list of times when Christian parents "bring their children to Jesus" for spiritual blessings.

Bible Discovery

[3]Behold, children are a heritage from the LORD, the fruit of the womb a reward.

[4]Like arrows in the hand of a warrior are the children of one's youth.

[5]Blessed is the man who fills his quiver with them!

He shall not be put to shame when he speaks with his enemies in the gate. Psalm 127:3–5

What's that Word? In Hebrew, "heritage" is *nachala,* which means "inheritance," something that can only be given as a gift from a giver to an heir. The land of Canaan is described as an "inheritance" for Israel (Numbers 34:2). Likewise, children are God's inheritance given to their parents and families.

What's that Word? In this passage, "reward" comes from the Hebrew word *sakar*, meaning "wages" or "hire." Children are both an unearned inheritance given as a gift *and* a reward. Jesus reminds us, "When you have done all that you were commanded, say, 'We are unworthy servants; we have only done what was our duty'" (Luke 17:10).

6. Psalm 127:3–5 also speaks of children as a blessing from God. In what way or ways do parents today show that they recognize children as God's blessing? In what way or ways is this blessing not recognized or even avoided?

7. Using an archery metaphor, the psalmist recounts the blessings of many children. While additional children in the household certainly take additional time, energy, and other resources, take a moment to consider the *positive* aspects of having several children in the Christian home. What are they?

Marriage in Real Life

8. Ken shares what his late father asked of him: "You make sure your children, my grandchildren, go to heaven." Which receives more attention today: children's physical and emotional needs or their spiritual needs? Why do you think this is so?

9. James and Becky talk about how the "big picture" (what's most important in marriage and parenting) can get lost. What are some things parents can do to keep God's "big picture" for their child in mind?

10. Glenn and Patti take an active role in their grandchildren's spiritual education. Besides the devotional books, prayer, and corporate worship that they mention, what else can grandparents do to support the spiritual growth of their grandchildren?

Teach the Children Diligently

Bible Discovery

4Hear, O Israel: The LORD our God, the LORD is one. 5You shall love the
LORD your God with all your heart and with all your soul and with all your
might. 6And these words that I command you today shall be on your heart.
7You shall teach them diligently to your children, and shall talk of them
when you sit in your house, and when you walk by the way, and when you
lie down, and when you rise. 8You shall bind them as a sign on your hand,
and they shall be as frontlets between your eyes. 9You shall write them on
the doorposts of your house and on your gates. Deuteronomy 6:4–9

What's that Word? In Hebrew, "heart" is *lebab*, which includes a person's entire emotions, intellect, and will. "Soul" is *nephesh*, which refers to a person's vitality and inner being. "Might" is *me'od*, which means force or strength. Taken together, these terms in Deuteronomy 6:5 represent the Lord's claim upon the entire person.

11. In the Hebrew, "teach them diligently" (v. 7) implies repetition, like sharpening a blade over and over again against a whetstone. Using the rest of verse 7, list those times when parents (and grandparents, aunts and uncles, and so on) can repeat God's Word to children.

"when you sit in your house" ______________________

"when you walk by the way" ______________________

"when you lie down" ______________________

"when you rise" ______________________

Bible Discovery

[4]We will not hide them from their children, but tell to the coming generation the glorious deeds of the LORD, and His might, and the wonders that He has done.

[5]He established a testimony in Jacob and appointed a law in Israel, which He commanded our fathers to teach to their children,

[6]that the next generation might know them, the children yet unborn, and arise and tell them to their children,

[7]so that they should set their hope in God and not forget the works of God, but keep His commandments. Psalm 78:4–7

What's that Word? The Hebrew word for "law" in Psalm 78:5 is *torah*, which means "teaching," or "instruction." It includes not only God's rules, but also the history of His saving deeds and His promises about the Messiah. *Torah* means both the Ten Commandments and the Good News of our Savior, Jesus Christ.

12. This passage from Psalm 78 illustrates the end to which God desires that His *torah* be taught to this generation and the next: so that they might be obedient to His commands and confident in His mercy. How can the promise of heaven help guide our actions when it comes to marriage and family issues? Consider 1 Timothy 2:3–4 before you answer.

Marriage in Real Life

13. Rather than approaching the subject legalistically, Ken and Amy suggest that the Church should emphasize God's design for marriage and the positive benefits of living according to His will. Do you agree? Why or why not?

14. In addition to worshiping together and good communication, Glenn suggests that couples set goals and "have fun." Why is "fun"—the creation of good experiences and positive, shared memories—so important in relationships?

____

____

____

____

15. David advises "enjoying the season" to those who are contemplating marriage, while Sharon notes the "learning curve" newlyweds experience. Discuss the benefits of a realistic, joy-filled approach to life.

____

____

____

____

We Are God's Children

Bible Discovery

14For all who are led by the Spirit of God are sons of God. 15For you did
not receive the spirit of slavery to fall back into fear, but you have received
the Spirit of adoption as sons, by whom we cry, "Abba! Father!" 16The
Spirit Himself bears witness with our spirit that we are children of God,
17and if children, then heirs—heirs of God and fellow heirs with Christ,
provided we suffer with Him in order that we may also be glorified with
Him. Romans 8:14–17

Family Language: Part 1

God uses family language to refer to Himself. He is the Rock, who fathered sons and daughters (Deuteronomy 32:18–19). "Have we not all one Father? Has not one God created us?" (Malachi 2:10). Jesus is both the Son of God (Luke 22:70) and the Son of Man (Matthew 9:6). God is the Father, the Son, and the Holy Spirit (Matthew 28:19).

Family Language: Part 2

God uses birth and adoption language to describe our entrance into His family. Through faith in His Son, Jesus Christ, we have become "children of God" (John 1:12). We have been born again by "water and the Spirit" (John 3:5). Through the Spirit, we have been "[adopted] as sons. . . children. . . heirs" (Romans 8:15–17).

16. "Abba" (Romans 8:15) is a childlike Aramaic term, like "papa" or "daddy," that conveys intimacy and confidence. How does knowing God is our heavenly Father help us when we pray, especially when we pray the words of the Lord's Prayer (Matthew 6:9–13)?

Closing Prayer

Heavenly Father, by Your grace in Jesus Christ You have given us new birth and adopted us as Your dear children. Renew our zeal for teaching the faith to children and all those you place in our care. By Your Spirit, preserve Your Word among us so that we might share it faithfully in blessing to all Your family, the Church. In Jesus' name. Amen.

This Week:

- "Children are a heritage." Commit to sponsoring a child through organizations such as World Vision, the Christian Children's Fund, or local child sponsorship opportunities.

- Review your answers to question 11. Select one and put it into practice by the end of the week.

- Confident in God, your heavenly Father, commit to praying for your spouse, children, and other family members by name on a daily basis.

Glossary

Abortion—The destruction of a human embryo or unborn fetus.

Adoption—Legally taking a child into one's family and raising him or her as one's own.

Bisexual—A person who engages in sexual acts with both males and females.

Chastity—Sexual self-control. Self-control is a gift; those who cannot live chaste lives as single persons are to marry.

Civil union—A legal contract between two parties recognized by some jurisdictions and extending certain legal rights and privileges traditionally reserved for married couples.

Conception—The process by which two gametes (sperm and oocyte, or egg) join their nuclear material to form a new, human person. Life begins at conception. See also *fertilization*.

Contraception—A combination of two words: *contra* (meaning "against") and *conception*. Any intentional prevention of conception or pregnancy through drugs, devices, or sexual practices.

Divorce—The legal dissolution of a marriage.

Fertilization—See *conception*. Some erroneously maintain that fertilization does not occur until an embryo implants itself in the womb or that embryos created *in vitro* are not fully human.

Heterosexual—A person who engages in sexual activity with another person of the opposite sex.

Homosexual—A person who engages in sexual activity with another person of the same sex.

Image of God—Righteousness and holiness before God enjoyed by human beings in full bodily and spiritual integrity prior to their fall into sin. God is restoring His image, the image of His Son, Jesus Christ, in believers through faith in Him. Jesus is the fullest image of God because He is God's Son.

***In vitro* fertilization**—Literally, "in a glass." The union of two human gametes (sperm and oocyte, or egg) in a laboratory to form a distinct human being. Typically, IVF necessitates the fertilization of multiple embryos, some of which may be frozen for later use, used in scientific research, or destroyed.

Lust—Any illicit sexual desire. Christians confess lust and all sin to the Lord, trusting in Christ for the forgiveness of their sins and for strength in fighting sexual temptation.

Marriage—The lifelong, one-flesh union of one man and one woman for the purposes of procreation, mutual love and help, and the legitimate channeling of natural, sexual desire.

Procreation—The participation of a married couple in the creative activity of God's command and blessing to "be fruitful and multiply." A comprehensive understanding of procreation includes conceiving, giving birth to, raising, and educating children in the ways of the Lord.

Reproduction—Biological term for human duplication. Exposes a limited, factory-like mentality of human generation that overlooks the duty to love, raise, and educate children. See *procreation*.

Same-sex marriage—Legal recognition of the sexual union of same-sex persons. Because marriage is the lifelong, one-flesh union of male and female, "same-sex marriage" is an oxymoron.

Sex—The male or female of a species; also the activity by which males and females engage their procreative organs.

Sex, according to the Bible—God created male and female with natural sexual desire for each other. He blesses chaste sexual activity only within His institution of marriage. Sinful sexual thoughts, words, and deeds arising from the heart, whether by a single or a married person, are condemned.

Sex, contemporary views—The work of Sigmund Freud (late-nineteenth to early-twentieth centuries) and Alfred Kinsey and Masters and Johnson (mid-twentieth century) personalized and emotionalized sex. Sex defines the individual; sexual activity is primarily for pleasure; marriage and family are social inventions.

Sexual intercourse, natural—In this course, the proper use (Romans 1:26–27) of the external male and female sex organs for the purpose of procreation (Genesis 1:28), strengthening the one-flesh union of husband and wife (Genesis 2:24), and properly channeling sexual desire (1 Corinthians 7:2).

Sexuality—In this course, that which relates to sexual activity.

Separation—A temporary or permanent condition between two married persons who cannot peacefully live in the same residence.